THE REMINISCENCES OF
Commander Norman H. Meyer
U.S. Naval Reserve (Retired)

INTERVIEWED BY
Paul Stillwell

U.S. Naval Institute • Annapolis, Maryland

Copyright © 2013

Preface

This oral history was the result of my friendship with the late Captain Slade Cutter, one of the U.S. Navy's most successful submarine captains during World War II. During one of our interviews, he mentioned that his 1935 Naval Academy classmate Norman Meyer had commanded a ship with a black crew during the war. That was the destroyer escort *Mason* (DE-529). In 1986 I embarked on a project that involved interviewing the then-living members of the Golden Thirteen, the Navy's first black officers, commissioned in 1944. One of the eight I interviewed was James Hair, who had been the first black officer to serve in the *Mason*. By happy coincidence, Commander Meyer was passing through Annapolis in the autumn of 1986, so I interviewed him about his experiences as well. In 1993 the Naval Institute Press published the book *The Golden Thirteen: Recollections of the First Black Naval Officers*. One of the chapters was drawn from the following interview with Meyer. He and I both did some editing of the raw transcript to arrive at the completed version.

Thanks go to Ms. Janis Jorgensen of the Naval Institute staff who has coordinated the printing and binding of the finished product.

In completing this volume, the Naval Institute expresses its gratitude to the Tawani Foundation and the Pritzker Military Library of Chicago for their generous financial support of the oral history program that produced this memoir.

Paul Stillwell
U.S. Naval Institute
September 2013

COMMANDER NORMAN HARRY MEYER
UNITED STATES NAVAL RESERVE (RETIRED)

Born: 24 August 1913 in St. James, Minnesota

Married: 6 July 1941 to Barbara Cleaveland Allen of Rockford, Illinois

Died: 24 June 2006 in Carlsbad, New Mexico at age 92

Naval Academy: 1931-35, served as third battalion commander and regimental commander (five-striper), business manager of the *Lucky Bag* yearbook and on the staff of *The Log* magazine

Dates of rank:

Ensign: 6 June 1935
Lieutenant (junior grade): 6 June 1940
Lieutenant: 1 June 1942
Lieutenant Commander: 1 July 1943
Commander: 20 July 1945

Active service:

USS *Lexington* (CV-2), 1935-36
USS *Barry* (DD-248), 1936-37
Temporary appointment revoked 5 June 1937 because of poor eyesight

Recalled to active duty: 14 March 1941
Pensacola Naval Air Station (instructor), 1941
USS *Saucy* (PG-65) (executive officer and commanding officer), 1942-43
Cruisers Destroyers Pacific Fleet (staff officer), 1943-45
USS *Mason* (DE-528) (commanding officer), 1945
Released from active duty: 18 December 1945

Retired from Naval Reserve: 1 August 1956

Authorization

The U.S. Naval Institute is hereby authorized to make available to individuals, libraries, and other repositories of its choosing the transcript of the oral history interview concerning the life and career of the undersigned. The interview was recorded on 6 November 1986 in collaboration with Paul Stillwell for the U.S. Naval Institute.

The undersigned does hereby release and assign to the U.S. Naval Institute all right, title, restrictions, and interest in the interview. The copyright in both the oral and transcribed version shall be the sole property of the U.S. Naval Institute. The tape recording of the interview is and will remain the property of the U.S. Naval Institute.

Signed and sealed this 16th day of February 1990.

Commander Norman H. Meyer, USNR (Ret.)

Interview with Commander Norman H. Meyer, U.S. Naval Reserve (Retired)
Place: U.S. Naval Institute, Annapolis, Maryland
Date: Thursday, 6 November 1986
Interviewer: Paul Stillwell

Paul Stillwell: To begin, could you please summarize your early background: your childhood and then going to the Naval Academy.

Commander Meyer: Well, I'm the seventh of 13 children, German blood descent. Mother lived to be 100. Dad lived to be almost 90, so I've got those marvelous, healthy genes.[*] I've got ten siblings still alive. We were in southern Minnesota, and we never had much money around for this big family.

Aside from good genes, Dad was a councilman once and had this sign, "I've accepted a public trust, and I will keep the faith," which symbolized his integrity. You know, if you accept a job, you do it. That's that!

Both of my parents were, in a quiet way, religious: good, solid Lutherans but tolerant. Mother had this absolute faith that God was in charge, and ultimately it would work out all right. They had bad times. Dad went bankrupt, there were problems in the family, we had to move, and so on. But they always had that deep faith in the Protestant ethic: work and things will be okay.

I was born in '13, and I vaguely remember World War I: the trains, the day at the end of the war they burned the Kaiser in effigy, and so on.[†] I vaguely remember that some of the super-bigoted patriots in that little town of St. James, Minnesota, threw yellow paint on some of our houses, because we were of German descent. I didn't react particularly. I think later on I felt, "What the hell?"

We were a big family, and a sort of tight family, I guess. Because of our economic status, we followed these health rules which people are coming to now. We had a big garden, we had cows, and we walked a lot. We dealt with farmers, and fruit,

---
[*] The interviewee's parents were Friederich August Diederich Karl Meyer and Bertha Anna Marie Uhlhorn Meyer.
[†] Kaiser Wilhelm II (1859-1941) was Emperor of Germany and King of Prussia from 1888 to 1918. Following the end of World War I in November 1918, he abdicated and lived the rest of his life in Holland.

and vegetables, and exercise. All my older brothers and sisters had to work to help the family eat, get along.

We lived in a little town, a good town. In the eighth grade, when I was 14, the Boy Scout organization came to town. That was a big thing for me. I remember a wonderful history teacher I had when President Coolidge was going to summer up in northern Wisconsin.* This teacher, Alice Sotagen, said, "Well, Norman, why don't you go up and say 'hello' to him?" So my buddy and I got out on this road and hitchhiked up there. Never saw Cal Coolidge, but it was the first of many adventures. Then through the scouts I helped build forest trails up where the Mississippi River starts, and canoed the Canadian border.

One of the men in the scout committee had a son who entered the class of '32 at the academy—Jack Seager.† While I was mowing his dad's tremendous lawn—the big man in the town—why, he started telling me about the Naval Academy. What he said aroused my interest, as though common people could go to this Valhalla of young men. Through the committeemen, who had political influence back when that was important, I got the appointment and got in. Actually, it was filled at the time, and then this Jack Seager out of '32 bilged out and left a vacancy. I just barely squeaked in.

Paul Stillwell: How ironic that you took his place.

Commander Meyer: I don't know whether he got kicked out because he was underweight or married, or both. He's still alive and lives in Severna Park.‡ Well, in effect, I had him and his wife as sponsors, which was very helpful to a scared kid.

So I entered the academy. I just squeaked in, because I was afraid that my eyes wouldn't be good enough. I passed the eye exam, but I was so scared my blood pressure went out of sight. So they rejected me and another, Jack O'Handley, who turned out to be my roommate for four years at the academy.§ Immediately the next day, his mother

---

* Calvin Coolidge was President of the United States from 1923 to 1929.
† Midshipman John W. Seager, USN. Seager later became an officer in the Navy's Supply Corps, retiring in 1960 as a commander.
‡ Severna Park, Maryland, is a small town between Annapolis and Baltimore.
§ John G. O'Handley graduated from the Naval Academy in the class of 1935 and eventually retired from active duty in 1957 as a captain.

came down from Jersey, took us two in tow. When we were rejected, we went over and appealed to the Surgeon General and sat around for two days—part of the psychology, just making you sit. She also went out to a drugstore and bought some narcotics, calmed us down. We got in.

Paul Stillwell: Had you been a good student in school in Minnesota?

Commander Meyer: Yes, I got sort of top grades, and I was president of the class and an Eagle Scout—all that stuff. There was a teachers' college across the street from the high school in Mankato. I went over there during study hour and took college math. The teachers, knowing I wanted to go to the academy, gave me a little bit of extra help. So I squeaked in—2.6 on the entrance exam.

Paul Stillwell: Were you the only member of your family, the siblings, that went to college?

Commander Meyer: I was the first. After me everyone went to college, except one younger brother who went in the National Guard before World War II as a buck private and came out as a major general.* One of my nephews now is in the Marines as an enlisted man. He was talking about it to me; he wanted to go to college. I said, "John, college is not the automatic. Look at your Uncle Paul, how successful this brother of mine has been." Now that Paul's retired, he's going to college to get his degree. But he was just a savvy guy.

My parents, of course, were intensely proud. I think once in a while of Slim Barham, who's written you about the *Laffey* and is a great guy.† He was a 2PO in our class, and I was five-striper.‡ He always refers to me as five-striper, so once I sort of quietly said to him, "You know, Slim, I'm very proud of what happened to a little boy 50 years ago. But it's 50 years ago." Not that I didn't want him to say it. And I said, "What

---
* Paul Victor Meyer was the name of the brother.
† Rear Admiral Eugene A. Barham, USN (Ret.), was a Naval Academy classmate of Meyer; Barham served in the destroyer *Laffey* (DD-459) during World War II.
‡ 2PO is the midshipman rank of second class petty officer; the five-striper was the regimental commander, the top rank at the time for a midshipman.

it really means to me, even to this day, is that my parents could be so proud of their son being five-striper at *the* Naval Academy. They deserved a boost in morale.

Dad had gone bankrupt. We had to move to a different town; he had to borrow money. Day by day, you know, it was touch and go in our family. There were some other troubles. A little sister died of scarlet fever, and the family had sort of real bad times. Suddenly their son went to the Naval Academy, which in those days was just like going to heaven.

Turns out there was another boy from the same town we moved to, Mankato. He was Johnny Flachsenhar, a classmate, whom I had known in scout camps.[*] He went at the same time, so there were two suddenly from the same town.

It made my parents feel very proud, of course, when I got to be five-striper. My good friend and classmate Nev Shaffer was chosen to be five-striper for the first three months of our senior year, and I was five-striper for the second three months.[†] Then Nev got to be five-striper for the final period while I stepped back to be a four-striper, commander of the third battalion. Nev deserved it, and I have to say I liked the more active role of a battalion commander. If you want to talk about honors, being business manager of one of the best *Lucky Bag*s ever published is what I am proudest of.[‡]

I ate the Naval Academy up. I think the second month I got a 4.0 in a calculus monthly exam. Next month another 4.0. I was off and running. From then on, I got star grades and it was easy.[§] Never was a big struggle except the eyes. I always had to worry about my eyes. The last year I had to pass the eye exam to be sure whether I'd get a commission or not. Went home for a month; didn't look at a newspaper. Came back and for six weeks didn't look at a book.

In our room in Bancroft Hall, there were two of us who got good grades and two anchormen.[**] We were roommates because we helped each other. They helped me learn

---

[*] Midshipman John J. Flachsenhar, USN, graduated from the Naval Academy in the class of 1935 and eventually retired as a captain in 1965.
[†] Midshipman John Nevin Shaffer, USN, graduated from the Naval Academy in the class of 1935 and eventually retired as a rear admiral in 1972.
[‡] *Lucky Bag* is the name of the Naval Academy yearbook.
[§] At the Naval Academy the midshipmen with the best academic ranking wear stars on the collars of their uniforms. Meyer stood number 28 of the 442 graduates in the class of 1935.
[**] Bancroft Hall is the Naval Academy dormitory; anchormen are the midshipmen near the bottom of the class standings.

how to drink beer and be human. And for six weeks I didn't look at a book—resting my eyes. Went to 9:00 o'clock English class and the professor said, "Well, now this morning we're going to read literature. Mr. Meyer, you'll read from Shakespeare." Just before the exam! Well, anyhow—so it was always a struggle as to whether I was going to stay in or not because of my eyes. At graduation, I got a conditional appointment as an ensign which, after two years was revoked because I had 14/20 in my right eye, and they needed 15/20.

Paul Stillwell: Awfully close.

Commander Meyer: Yes, but those were the rules, and I never felt bitter. That's the chance I took. I play by the rules usually, unless I think I can get away with a little innocent fudging.

Paul Stillwell: Well, really, it was to the Navy's detriment that, having invested this education in you, they didn't take advantage of it.

Commander Meyer: Oh, sure, well, they said, "Go in the Supply Corps." Well, hell, I've never been very good at figures, and it would have ruined my eyes to be in supply. If I'd thought earlier, I might have gone in what we called the Construction Corps in those days.* But, anyhow, I had two great years: a year in the carrier *Lexington* and a year in the destroyer *Barry*.

Then I got out and got a job in industry. The boss at Bakelite that I got a job from had been at the Naval Academy for a couple years. He was Rupe Lowe of the class of 1922, so we had that sort of nice relationship.†

So I think that's as much as I can tell you about my early background.

---

* The Construction Corps was disestablished just before World War II. Its members were then redesignated engineering duty officers (EDOs). Often drawn from those who finished at the top of their Naval Academy classes, the naval constructors were involved in the technical aspects of designing and building ships.

† Rupert B. Lowe resigned from the service prior to commissioning. The class of 1922 had entered the Naval Academy in 1918, during World War I. Following the conclusion of "the war to end all wars," members of the class were encouraged to resign because of the belief that they would not have a viable career in a much-reduced Navy.

Paul Stillwell: What sort of work did you do from then until you were recalled to active duty?

Commander Meyer: Well, I was a factory supervisor at Bound Brook, New Jersey. Bakelite was bringing out a new type of plastics raw material.* I was young enough so that I could walk into hot ovens and do some experiments—chemical engineering experimenting—and yet I had a college education. I was what you'd call today a process development engineer, sort of an efficiency expert working out the bugs. I remember as a young bachelor living an hour from New York City, sitting in Carnegie Hall on a Sunday afternoon—New York Philharmonic—and working out problems in my head that I'd apply at the plant on Monday.

I was a bachelor there and lived in a crazy boarding house for a year. The food was so wretched, one of the other guys and I used to go up to his room and have a belt or two of bourbon in order to put the food down. Finally, he said, "I wish I knew somebody who could cook, we'd rent an apartment.

I said, "I got the cooking merit badge. I know how to fry pancakes." And with three other guys, we rented a house up in the hills of New Jersey and lived like an adult fraternity house. Of course, the word was that we had naked women at the spring. We didn't have a spring, and we didn't have any naked women, but we might have thought about it. Then it came time to sign up for the draft. We lived in sort of farming country, and we six handsome young guys went around to a schoolhouse and signed up. They thought, "Oh, this is fine." And they said, "Are you married?"

"No. We live at a boarding house, and so-and-so."

They were very warm until suddenly they decided we were six queers. We got hustled out of there.

But I lived near New York, and enjoyed going to the opera, standing up for a dollar, and seeing Helen Hayes and 90-cent dinner in Times Square.† Great time to be a bachelor there in the New York area.

---

* The Bakelite Corporation was founded in 1922. In 1939 Union Carbide and Carbon Corporation bought out Bakelite.
† Helen Hayes was a prominent American actress, both on the stage and in movies.

Paul Stillwell: Had the condition of your eyes changed any in the meantime?

Commander Meyer: Not really, no. All my life they've been sort of touch and go. Even to this day, they bother me a little bit, but it's of no consequence.

After three and a half years, one of my roommates, Dick McGowan—who was lost in the war, an aviator—wrote to me in the fall of '40.[*] France had just fallen, and it was obvious that we were going to get in the war. He said, "Norm, we need guys like you to teach these smart-ass college kids how to be an officer in four weeks, which it took us dummies at Annapolis four years to learn." He said, "I wish you'd come to Pensacola and teach these aviation cadets and be, you know, their duty officer."

So I volunteered and went back in the Navy on March 14 of '41—well before Pearl Harbor. In that last month, I met this redhead in New York on a blind date. We were engaged in ten days; it was a whirlwind courtship. Then I went off to Pensacola. And three months later, I drove up to Rockford, Illinois, and I married this strange woman that I hardly knew. But we're still married after 45 good years.

Paul Stillwell: That's great.

Commander Meyer: Yes.

Paul Stillwell: So what rank did you come back as?

Commander Meyer: As a jaygee.[†] And made $196.00 a month, every month.

Paul Stillwell: Did you have the same seniority as your classmates?

Commander Meyer: No, I dropped two classes. I had seniority with '37, which, of course, really meant nothing to me, because I had no idea of a career in the Navy. Even

---

[*] Lieutenant (junior grade) Richard McGowan, USN. McGowan had finished 434th of the 442 graduates in the Naval Academy's class of 1935. McGowan was killed 24 October 1944 in a plane crash during the Battle of Leyte Gulf.
[†] Jaygee – lieutenant (junior grade).

later, when I went to the *Mason*, people said, "It'll ruin your professional reputation."*

I said, "My reputation's back at a factory in New Jersey. I'm just trying to get this war over with, and that's my aim in life—to get back to my wife and a baby I hardly know." So I ranked with '37. Of course, by the end of the war I made commander.

Paul Stillwell: Well, I'm interested. Why was there a perception that you would ruin your reputation? You mean within the Navy?

Commander Meyer: Well, you see, my Naval Academy classmates sort of considered me regular Navy, even though I really came back as a reservist. Well, if you get a bad ship and you can't do anything with it, you get hung with the reputation of that ship.

Paul Stillwell: Was there an assumption that it would be a bad ship because it had a black crew?

Commander Meyer: Well, it was a bad ship, period. It really was—but not because of the color of the skin of the crew. It was just so obvious to any experienced officer. I said, "I relieve you, sir." The previous captain left, probably glad to go. We had no interchange at all. I took over and set to work, not bothering too much to look back or worry about things done and gone. I felt there had been a lack of adequate leadership from top down. The executive was a wonderful navigator but had not been effective as far as I could see. The next senior was the gunnery officer, and I was not impressed.

One of the first things I did after taking command was to tell the crew, "You are not Negro sailors. You are American fighting men. I'll expect the same from you as anybody else who's ever served under me. And I'll fight for you the same way that I have fought for others who have served under me." My expectation was, of course, not only that I believed in their potential, but I was damn well going to make sure that they lived up to that potential.

---

* On 12 June 1945, Meyer became commanding officer of the USS *Mason* (DE-529), a destroyer escort.

Paul Stillwell: What were the intermediate steps between Pensacola and getting command of the ship?

Commander Meyer: I was at Pensacola about a year. Finally, Barbara got pregnant and—boom—I got orders to leave Pensacola the next day and get in our car and drive in February of '42 to Boston. We got there, and someone said, "We don't know why, but there have been 45 other people here ahead of you. Go back to 90 Church Street, New York, on Monday."* I got in a room there in New York, and it turned out they were assembling crews—officers and men—to go to England in, I think, the second convoy of American troops. We were trying to guard the East Coast of the United States with four converted yachts. Of course, the German submarines were having a field day. So the British gave us ten of these corvettes—antisubmarine escort vessels. One of them was already in the Brooklyn Navy Yard; it had blown up its boiler off of Halifax.

So we went over to the other side and stayed there until the ships were refitted. We took over these nine ships and sailed them back across the Atlantic, then went south to the Caribbean and South Atlantic on escort duty. I was exec at first, and then I became captain.

Paul Stillwell: What ship was that?

Commander Meyer: That was the *Saucy*, corvette, 85 men in the crew.† It was built on a whaler hull and tossed and pitched and so on, so it just kept you in shape just to hold on to the damn thing. I was exec for a year.

As I was telling one of my classmates, "My life has had many bright spots. It's had some rather dark spots too." During that time in the *Saucy*, I went through my first depression. Actually, if you want to know the honest-to-God truth, I deserted as an officer in wartime, for which you could get shot. I came out of Annapolis with illusions

---

* The headquarters building for the Third Naval District was at 90 Church Street in New York City.
† USS *Saucy* (PG-65) was 205 feet long, had a beam of 33 feet, draft of 15 feet, speed of 16.5 knots, and displacement of 925 tons. She was commissioned as a U.S. Navy ship at Belfast, Ireland, on 30 April 1942 with Lieutenant Andrew J. Smith, USN, in command.

about perfection and duty and performance, and the skipper of this ship just couldn't fit my ideas of what an officer should be. (I didn't fit his ideas either.)

When we got to Boston, I finally just threw up my hands, left the ship, and said, "I can't do this anymore." My wife had come east from Illinois, being very pregnant. I went out to Beacon Hill, where we had rented an apartment, and I said, "I'm done. I quit. I quit."

Fortunately, the officer who'd been division commander on the destroyer that I served on right out of Annapolis a year was in Boston as a captain at that time. Barbara knew him and called him, and said, "Captain, what'll I do? This is my husband; he is helpless."

Paul Stillwell: Who was he?

Commander Meyer: Captain Wilder D. Baker—great guy.*

Well, they hustled me over to Chelsea Naval Hospital. I remember being admitted, and one nurse said, "What's the matter? This is assigned for mental patients." I got in the hands of this wonderful civilian doctor who'd become a naval psychiatrist, Bob Schwab, who later did a lot of Parkinson's disease research.†

He said, "Oh, Norm, why don't you and Barbara come down to Cape Cod and spend a weekend with us." Monday we got in his office, and he said, "You know, there's nothing wrong with you. You just set too-high standards. Why don't you come on down to earth with the rest of us human beings?" He said, "You tied that boat up as though it were a battleship. Your standards are too high. And as far as the captain is concerned, learn to swear like he does. Then go on back to your ship. You and your wife have a life to lead."

That was before the days of the tranquilizers and so on, which I later have been treated by. I must say the longest hundred yards I ever walked in my life was down the dock at Guantánamo to rejoin my ship.‡ All the enlisted men were looking and probably

---

* Captain Baker was then Commander Destroyer Squadron 31.
† Lieutenant Robert S. Schwab, Medical Corps, USNR.
‡ Guantánamo Bay, on the south coast of Cuba, near the eastern end of the island, for many years provided a fleet anchorage and training area for U.S. Navy ships.

thinking, "Here's that great Lieutenant Meyer who quit." Because they all knew what had happened.

I came on board, assumed my duties, and learned to swear. I heard the captain one day listening to me saying, "Goddamn."

He said, "Meyer's a pretty good officer now." That was his standard.

One night we were cruising with a convoy in the dark. I was standing where I could hear a bunch of enlisted men bullshitting, and one said, "One of these days Lieutenant Meyer's going to be captain."

And this boatswain's mate said, "If he ever does, I'll jump over the side." I wasn't winning popularity contests with everybody. But I got to be captain and made it a good ship. That's a ship that's another story that I'm using as the basis for this musical play for kids that I've been at work on.

Anyhow, I had that command. One of our actions was to rescue a tanker that displaced ten times as much as we did—towed it 125 miles to the shore of Brazil. For that we received a commendation. Previously we had been convoying some ships and just off the Amazon we spotted a periscope at 4:00 P.M. Through the night we kept dropping depth charges, but because the water was so shallow, the force of the explosions impacted on us, and we did ourselves more damage than the sub.[*]

At 7:00 the next morning, we sighted the telltale bubbles of a torpedo fired at us. Before I could order, "Hard right rudder," helmsman Bud Morgan had the ship swinging. That probably saved us as the torpedo went whistling close aboard. After I tightened my life preserver, I exclaimed, "That guy is serious; he's trying to kill us." Twenty minutes later, there was another torpedo and then a third—after which we lost contact.

One of the things I did was to give the men ice cream, and hand-crank phonographs, which I found at Belém, way up the Amazon.[†] They got music, records, and so on, and then a bulletin board. I said, "You can put anything you want on it as long

---

[*] The rush of fresh water at the mouth of the Amazon creates layers that reflect sonar echoes. In discussing the attack made by the Saucy on 22-23 March 1943, Samuel Eliot Morison wrote the following on page 389 of his *The Battle of the Atlantic, 1939-1943* (Boston: Little, Brown, 1947): "This attack failed because Saucy made eleven false contacts on tide-rips off the mouth of the Amazon, chased them all night, and was damaged by her own depth charges. A submarine was present, but escaped."

[†] Belém, Brazil, is at the entrance to the Amazon River.

as it's not obscene or unpatriotic." They'd write letters and poems. You know, enlisted men have a lot of talent. They're great guys.

On one Friday inspection there was a cartoon on rough paper, showing all the armament going off at the same time. Underneath it said, "The Mighty Battleship *Saucy*." In other words, this guy was kidding me, saying, "The Captain thinks he's in charge of a battleship. It's nothing but a little corvette."

I turned it over and could tell by his writing who'd done it. So I called him up, and he was scared. But I said, "No, don't be afraid. Just two things: will you draw me a smooth copy?"—which he did—and then I said, "You think you've got all the armament going off at once, but you forgot the captain's .45." So he drew me in there with my .45. (It is framed and hangs in my study.)

An officer that I knew and loved was sunk on the *Laffey*. It turns out it was the skipper of the *Laffey*, and Slim Barham was on there.[*] I said, "I'm not needed here on this. I've got a good exec who can take over, Henry Doyle."[†] I got transferred to the Pacific and was on a staff in the Pacific for those two years as training officer.

Paul Stillwell: Of what command?

Commander Meyer: Commander Cruisers Destroyers Pacific Fleet. It was an administrative command entirely. Any battleship, cruiser, destroyer, or destroyer escort that entered Pearl Harbor was given to my admiral boss for administration.

Paul Stillwell: Was that Admiral Kauffman?

Commander Meyer: First it was Tisdale, then Kauffman.[‡] Kauffman had it for most of the time. Of course, as a lieutenant and lieutenant commander, I was a guy that would go out and visit the ship, and I'd say, "Captain, you're going to be in port for ten days.

---

[*] Lieutenant Commander William E. Hank, USN, was the commanding officer of the destroyer *Laffey* when she was sunk in a night battle off Guadalcanal the night of 12-13 November 1942.
[†] Lieutenant Henry G. Doyle, Jr., USNR.
[‡] Rear Admiral Mahlon S. Tisdale, USN, was Commander Cruisers Pacific Fleet from April 1943 to January 1944; concurrently he was Commander Destroyers Pacific Fleet from January 1943 to January 1944; Rear Admiral James L. Kauffman, USN, held both billets simultaneously from January to October 1944.

You've got two days in which we're going to hold school for your officers, so let the enlisted men go ashore and beer up, and so on. And what kind of training do you want?"

Then I'd go back with my group of Yale and Harvard 90-day wonders, and work out the schedule, and write out the orders, while the admiral was entertaining the captain over at the O-club, which was fine.* That was my contribution to the war effort, because I'm a pretty good administrator. After a while, I got so I could tell whether a ship could shoot almost within the first five minutes on board, whether the gangway watch was sharp and neatly dressed, whether dirt was in the corner, whether the man on watch knew where the captain was, and so on.

So it was an interesting sort of a job. Of course, after a while some of my classmates would say, "Norm, your lectures would have more of a tinge of authenticity if you'd ever been out to the Western Pacific." Which I hadn't, but I'd fought that submarine and so on. So I got a chance to go out on a destroyer at the Peleliu invasion and on a carrier, fast carrier task force.† Admiral Baker, you see, was Admiral McCain's chief of staff.‡ I'd finished my two months' assignment in one month, and I was about to go back to Pearl. Admiral Baker met me at this long bar at Manus, and he said, "What are you doing?" So I told him.

He said, "Well, Norm, I can't tell you what we're going to do, but we're going to have an interesting time. Why don't you just come along?" So I got permission to ride along and got in on some of the early strikes against Okinawa and Formosa. Then back to Pearl.

It was getting time for me to go to sea, and that's when I picked up the Myrdal book that the Carnegie Corporation had financed, *An American Dilemma*.§

Paul Stillwell: Why did you pick it up at that point?

---

* Reserve officers trained in short-term programs were known as "90-day wonders." O-club – officers' club.
† U.S. Marines invaded the island of Peleliu, in the Palau group, in mid-September 1944.
‡ Rear Admiral Wilder D. Baker, USN, was chief of staff to Vice Admiral John S. McCain, USN, Commander Task Force 58. McCain's flagship was the aircraft carrier *Wasp* (CV-18).
§ Gunnar Myrdal was a Swedish economist whose book was *An American Dilemma: The Negro Problem and Modern Democracy* (New York: Harper & Row Publishers, Inc., 1944).

Commander Meyer: Well, I was not a geographical bachelor; you know, I was a good boy. I didn't chase around with women, so I had lots of nights free. I read a great deal. *Time* magazine had a review of this Myrdal book, and it piqued my interest. So I sent away and got the big two volumes of it and read it through. It opened my eyes.

Then, thinking that they had several DEs with a black crew, I wrote to Eddie Fahy, who was a detail officer in the Navy.* I said, "Eddie, I'm due to go to sea and take command of a destroyer escort. While I'm doing that, since I'm a lay person in the Navy anyhow, I am willing to be captain of one of these Negro ships," because I sensed that it was probably not a job that people would go for.

He wrote back and said, "We got one, and it's a mess. If you want it, you can have it." Quickly people warned me that it was a national disgrace—one of Eleanor Roosevelt's crazy ideas—and black people won't fight, they're cowards, they'll run, and all sorts of things.† And I just by then was confident enough of my ability as an officer that I said, "I think I can swing it. I'll take it."

Paul Stillwell: What had been your general attitude toward blacks before you read the book?

Commander Meyer: Well, you know, just sort of blank. We didn't have many blacks in Minnesota. When I entered the Naval Academy that first day, Jack O'Handley and I moved in with these two classmates from Georgia and Florida. Of course, we all opened up our high school annuals. Jack's had black classmates. One of these kids from the South said, "My God, you mean you went to school with those people?"

I didn't know anything about them, and, of course, they told me, "Well, niggers can't think; their heads are just solid unless they have some white blood. Then their skull sort of opens up; they can't grow intellectually,"—you know, all the clichés. They said, "We know, because we've lived with them all our lives. You Northerners don't know because you've never had niggers around you."

---

* DEs – destroyer escorts. Actually the USS *Mason* was the only destroyer escort with a black crew. The detail officer was Commander Edward J. Fahy, USN.
† Eleanor Roosevelt was the socially conscious wife of President Franklin D. Roosevelt.

So mentally I was sort of a blank. The only blacks I saw at Annapolis were the janitors that cleaned the corridors or the first classmen's rooms. I didn't see any bright, educated Negroes. I just saw the lower end of the spectrum, so that reinforced what my Southern friends had said, that they were inferior, hardly human beings. Of course, we heard the terrible clichés: "niggers," and "jigaboos," and all of that.

Even Jack Seager, who's from Minnesota, who helped me get in, had had that same attitude about blacks. It was just not to be questioned. I think I did question it in my own mind, but I kept my mouth shut, because I had no basis. During the years that I was a bachelor, I recall going to a party in New York City, and the most attractive gal there was a young black woman, bright and so on. So I was just sort of neutral about it, but I think I began to wonder whether it was really true. With the name Meyer, once in a while I was mistaken for a Jew. And occasionally I experienced a little bit of anti-Semitism. I had some very bright, attractive Jewish classmates, and I thought, "Oh, what the hell! This isn't right."

Paul Stillwell: So you had a bit of sympathy then.

Commander Meyer: I was sort of neutral but sympathetic. It just seemed to me what counted was what people were, but I never articulated it until I read that book.

Paul Stillwell: That was a real eye-opener, it sounds like.

Commander Meyer: Oh, that was a watershed to me. Then the Army at that time was trying to integrate Negroes into their troops, and it had lectures and pamphlets there in Hawaii. I began to get interested in it and accumulated some of that material.

Then one of the illusions I had was that I should learn how to teach black people to read and write. So I was going to get the materials, and somebody who knew about the DE, the *Mason*, said, "Don't worry. Those are a very select bunch of Negroes in that crew."

When I got on board the Mason, it was obvious right away this was a poorly performing ship.* As I said, in that job in Pearl Harbor I could walk on board and in five minutes tell whether a ship could shoot. We would later on send them down to the shooting range. We'd measure their ability to shoot, and it correlated.

The *Mason* simply was not a good ship.† For instance, we'd get ready to get under way, when ordinarily the exec would come up and say, "Captain, ship's ready to get under way." But it wasn't ready; some line was still holding us to the dock, or somebody hadn't finished some requirement. So I saw I had work to do. To get acquainted with the crew, I asked one chief petty office and one officer after the other to come to my cabin for a cup of coffee and to talk.

Paul Stillwell: You still had all white officers at that point, didn't you?

Commander Meyer: Yes. I remember one who was from Texas. He said, "Captain, I've been on this for 18 months, and I know what you're going to do. You're going to get black officers on board. I'm all for it. I'd like to stay, but my dad is a politician in Texas, and if they ever heard down there that I eat at the same table with black people, my dad would be dead."

So I said, "Well, you've done your tour." And I got him transferred.

But I talked with the exec and gunnery officer, and they just verbally fenced with me. Finally, when I talked to John Phillips, who was the fourth-ranking officer, he exploded all of a sudden.‡ He said, "Oh, Captain, I couldn't stand to be in the same room with your predecessor. He's such a repulsive, alcoholic, incompetent officer. I've been trying desperately to get off this ship."

---

* The ship was named for Ensign Newton H. Mason, USNR, an aviator in Fighting Squadron Three; he died following aerial combat against the Japanese in the Battle of the Coral Sea in May 1942. The USS Mason had a standard displacement of 1,140 tons. She was 289 feet long, 35 feet in the beam, and had a draft of 8 feet. Her top speed was 21 knots. She was armed with three 3-inch guns and various antiaircraft and antisubmarine weapons.

† For a different perspective on this issue, see Mary Pat Kelly, *Proudly We Served: the Men of the USS Mason* (Annapolis: Naval Institute Press, 1995). The book covers the ship's entire World War II service, including the time when Meyer's predecessor was the commanding officer.

‡ Lieutenant (junior grade) John C. Phillips, USNR.

So I was smart enough to recognize his ability. I called Eddie Fahy in the Navy Department the next day, and I said, "Eddie, I want him to be exec, and transfer these other two off the ship." So I had a fairly junior exec, but he was a lawyer, with a law degree from Penn State, just very solid. I'm sort of impatient and such like, and he was a very steadying influence.

Then we were putting in to the Earle ammunition depot there near Sandy Hook.[*] The tug which was helping us dock was really sharp. The brass literally shone and sparkled; the ship handling and everything else were excellent. Everybody on board was black, and it was Jim Hair's ship.[†] It turned out Jim had been enlisted quartermaster on a tug before he went to officer school, so he knew tugs. I was so impressed by his tug that I invited him over lunch. I had the Myrdal book handy when he came aboard. He and his crew were very proud, because here was this lieutenant commander inviting him to lunch: "The boss is going to go over there with those white folks."

The next day, when I called Eddie Fahy to say I wanted Hair to be my first lieutenant, the crew wasn't so happy, because I was stealing their real nice skipper. From then on, we took off, and what happened on the ship is pretty well recounted in an article I wrote.[‡]

Paul Stillwell: Well, I'd like to get it in here in more detail. I was struck by your comment about the quality of the crew. I talked to Judge White, one of the Golden Thirteen men, and he felt that the *Mason* and *PC-1264* were shortchanged, that various commands had been designated to send black men to crew these ships.[§] He said they wouldn't send their best ones; they'd keep those for themselves. Now, did you feel you got a fair cross-section of talent?

---

[*] The ammunition depot is at Earle, New Jersey, not far from New York City.
[†] Ensign James E. Hair, USNR, was in Navy's first group of black commissioned officers. He was the skipper of *YTB-215*, a yard tugboat assigned to the Third Naval District. Hair spelled his name "Hare" during his time in the Navy, for reasons he explains in his own Naval Institute oral history.
[‡] The article was published subsequent to this interview as "Jim Hair and USS Mason," pages 17-18 of the March 1990 issue of *Shipmate*, the monthly magazine of the U.S. Naval Academy Alumni Association.
[§] William Sylvester White is a member of the Golden Thirteen. His oral history is in the Naval Institute collection. The *PC-1264* was the Navy's other ship, in addition to the *Mason*, with a black crew during World War II. A number of harbor craft, such as James Hair's, had black crews.

Commander Meyer: I never stopped to question. They were my crew, and there were enough of them. I suppose there were 150. I don't go wearing it on my sleeve, but Albert Schweitzer's "reverence for life" expresses my attitude toward the people who work for me, whether sailors, factory workers, or supervisors.* They put their time, effort, their soul into working for me. I should care enough to help them develop to the maximum. And caring takes many forms—not just being nice and thoughtful but also being pretty firm. It is my philosophy of management.

As I said to those guys, "You're American fighting men." And we went to work. I got rid of the officers that weren't up to what I thought they should be, and got Jim Hair and John Phillips. We got another black officer later on, a young ensign who was just like any other.

There were some crew members that were miserable, of course. One of them in particular is an example. He came up to captain's mast and, hell, he had a string of offenses.† Whatever punishment I gave him that time is irrelevant, but I said, "You know, if you do this again, I'm not going to do anything to you."

"Oh no, sir, no?"

I said, "You're going to do it to yourself. You're going to kick yourself right out of the Navy."

"Oh, don't worry, Captain, I'll never be up here." Three weeks later he was up at mast again. I said, "Well, Johnny, you remember our talk of three weeks ago?"

"Yes, sir, Captain."

And I said, "I wasn't going to do anything."

"Yes, sir, Captain."

"That you were going to do something."

"Yes, sir, Captain."

"You're going to kick yourself out of the Navy. Well, you just did." I suspected he wanted to get out of the Navy anyway. I suppose there were a few others that we got rid of.

---

* Dr. Albert Schweitzer (1876-1965) was a French clergyman, physician, and musical scholar who worked for many years as a missionary in Africa. He was awarded the Nobel Peace Prize in 1952.
† Captain's mast is the Navy's non-judicial punishment, administered by the commanding officer of a unit rather than by a court-martial.

What's new about this is that some of the men were excellent. Our sound team that operated the sonar was superb, just superb. Of course, some people say, "Colored people are good at music." Whether it's true or not, it's the area where they've been able to make a living.

And the rest of them—for instance, our engineering officer, Lieutenant Anderson, was a wonderful engineer, and he had a hell of a good back gang.* Our communication officer, as I recollect, was sort of marginal, so we had a marginal communication group.

Paul Stillwell: Performance really was a product of the leadership.

Commander Meyer: The leadership and opportunity. It was like the bell curve. Those who were so good, they'd be good anywhere. And those who were so useless, they couldn't be good anywhere. So what? Profound truth.

Paul Stillwell: Did you have a means through your exec, who was a holdover, of measuring the comparison of morale in the crew from your predecessor to yourself?

Commander Meyer: We had three busy, busy months. We went through drills and drills. We didn't spend much time philosophizing like that. We just worked as hard as we could on training. And I think it was obvious that things were improving. The crew noticed when I got rid of those officers who weren't very good. Then whenever one of the men would get promoted, I'd write a letter to his parents or his wife. Under wartime censorship, they couldn't tell too much of what they'd been doing. I'd say, "Dear Mrs. Jones, your son Johnny serves on my ship. He has been promoted to signalman third class, and I want to congratulate him." Second paragraph I would sort of outline his duties. Third paragraph I'd say, "I'm proud to have him serve underneath me, and you can be proud of his contribution to the war effort."

I don't think anything I did was so gratifying and brought such good rewards, because I got nice letters back from the families and, you know, it showed. I believed in

---

* Lieutenant William Anderson, USNR. "Black gang" is a traditional Navy term for the men who run a ship's propulsion plant; it has nothing to do with the race of the individual crew members.

performance. It was like when I was teaching aviation cadets before the war. I had four weeks to teach them about being officers before they went on to learn to fly. I was rough. I would get up early, hide, and then put them on report for walking on the grass. But at the end of the war some of them came to me, and they said, "You saved my life. You taught me that when somebody said 'go right,' you don't stop and scratch your ass. You go right."

So I had high standards of performance, and so did the other officers. On the other hand, I think an officer should take care of his people. I got involved when some of them were in trouble; it was my job. After all, the material was there, and John Phillips and Jim Hair were two outstanding helpers.

Paul Stillwell: Could you describe their individual contributions?

Commander Meyer: Well, of course, Jim had been an enlisted man. He was black. He'd had command of that tug; he'd been to officer school. And he's a very bright guy. He's very intelligent, intensely patriotic. He was proud to be black and extremely proud to have come to our ship. He felt this was a real honor.

Paul Stillwell: Well, it was a reward for good performance.

Commander Meyer: Sure it was, and I'm sure he communicated that. If the enlisted men had some doubts about this honky Meyer, he could tell them that I was sincere. I was really interested in performance but also in their concerns. You know, Norwegians can communicate with Norwegians better than anybody else probably. And I felt, much as I liked and respected blacks, I could never quite communicate as well as a black. So Jim Hair was that medium. He believed in me and what we were trying to do, and in high performance, so that was very helpful.

As an example of the sort of person John Phillips was, as a lawyer he went back to Philadelphia. He was very much instrumental in one of the perennial cleanups of corruption in the city of Philadelphia, and was on his way to becoming prominent in

Pennsylvania politics where he could have been governor. Finally, he said, "Norm, I can't stomach the sort of people that the politicians have to associate with."

He left that and went to work for the Insurance Company of North America, which is now a part of the CIGNA group. He became a vice president, a very senior, prominent, and successful insurance executive. He's just a hell of a bright guy. He and I made a good team. He liked me, I liked him, and we worked things out together. He was the ideal exec, because I was full of ideas, and every once in a while I'd get a wild hair up my ass, and he'd say, "Captain, I don't really think that's a good idea. Let's not push things too fast, too far."

The other officers we had on board supported us. And then we got another black officer.

Paul Stillwell: Who was he?

Commander Meyer: Ensign McIntosh.* I think we can probably find him someplace. Jim Hair and I are going to undertake to find the crew and see if we can have a reunion in a year or two. We got four ensigns at one time, as I recollect. Three were white and one was black. All were confused and green.

Paul Stillwell: Well, you mentioned when you first went aboard that you could tell this was not a smart ship, and you had the high standards. So it had to be a matter that the crew had to adjust to you.

Commander Meyer: Oh, yes. There was no question. I was going to make them toe the line. I wasn't going to lower my expectations. I just thought, "You're sailors. You're going to stand the same standards that anybody else does." I expected that they could, and I was going to damn well insist that they did. After all, when you compare me with the first skipper: I'd been through the Naval Academy. I'd had two years as an officer in the fleet. I'd had command of a ship earlier in the war.

---

* Ensign John McIntosh, USNR.

Incidentally going back to the *Saucy*, blacks had become sort of an important thing in my life, and in each of those crews that were sent to Ireland there were two black men: an officers' steward and an officers' cook. These black guys—two times nine ships equals 18—convinced the Irish gals that they were American Indians. They were very successful. You know what—American enlisted men, they're the greatest, you know, very resourceful. They persuaded the Irish gals that if you did it standing up, you didn't get pregnant. So walking down the streets in Londonderry, all these inset doors, there was a hell of a lot of vertical action going on. I bet there were a lot of little American babies even so.

There were two black guys on the *Saucy*; one was big old Hunter. Instead of having separate food for the officers and food for the enlisted men, I said, "We're going to have one mess. Hunter, you cook for the whole crew, and so we can use the ship's cook for something else." He was really good. They were just good people.

Paul Stillwell: Well, and you'd had the training tour of duty in which you must have had a lot of those ideas from seeing how other ships did this. Now here was a chance to implement them.

Commander Meyer: Oh, yes. Oh, yes. I had the right background for the job, and it would have been a disgrace if I had not proceeded moderately well with the *Mason*.

Paul Stillwell: Was it your feeling that you got a fair cross-section of the talent that could be expected in a ship of that size?

Commander Meyer: Well, frankly, until you asked me, Paul, those thoughts never occurred to me that we didn't. As I mentioned, I have this great respect for the American enlisted men. I think they're, by and large, great guys. You have all this talent, and if you just give them a break and some training, they'll do anything for you. The real enlisted men will do anything for a good officer; they're tremendously loyal. It's just that team. It works two ways: you take care of them, they take care of you.

Paul Stillwell: Well, you must have had a few recalcitrants because you've told me about snipping off shirttails.

Commander Meyer: Oh, well, yes. That was not one of my brighter days, I guess. Sure, I had these crazy ideas. I didn't like people going around with shirttails out. So I had scissors with me and I'd snip them off square. And the damn radio gang had charge of the public address system, in which they played records all day. Well, I decreed no one record could be played more than ten times in 24 hours.

Paul Stillwell: That's a reasonable directive.

Commander Meyer: I thought it was reasonable—not to tighten down.

The factory where I worked before the war was right there in New Jersey, and when I came from all this fighting in the Pacific, I visited them, and they said to me, in effect, "Gee, Norm, we admire you. You're out there fighting the war and winning this war, and we really haven't done our part. We've been deferred and working here."

I said, "Hell, we couldn't win this war without this tremendous industrial production. Tell you what, I'm going to take my ship out for a day's run, and you be in Dock so-and-so in Brooklyn Tuesday on Wednesday at 8:00 o'clock. You can see for yourself how valuable the plastics you have been making are to the war effort—how my ship could not run without them."

Paul Stillwell: Were they from the Bakelite Company?

Commander Meyer: Yes. Just the afternoon before, I'd gotten permission to go out. Because I wanted to go through a whole lot of drills—drills, drills, drills, drills, drills all day long. They said, "Well, we've got a cameraman that wanted to take some pictures the other day and didn't finish. He'd like to go along." I envisaged some guy with a little bit of a Brownie.

We waited at the dock. Finally, two tremendous big sound trucks straight from Hollywood and a director with a checkered cap and everything came on board. They wanted to make a sound short to the tune, "Bell Bottom Trousers, Coats of Navy Blue." Complete with all of their equipment, they got on board. I put them on the forecastle gun, and all day long they were going over, and over, and over again. Well, then we were going through one drill after the other with the crew.

These eight Bakelite engineers scampered all over the ship. I remember old Paul Parmalee went to the top of the mast. Coming down, the whistle blew. He started up, it stopped, went down again, it blew again. He did it three times before he realized his ass was catching on the whistle cord. Then we had practice going—landing against a cardboard box—and swim call. It was quite a day. Like John Phillips said, "I bet the U.S. Navy's never seen a day like this before or since."

It was training, and it was fun. One of the pleasures I had as captain was bringing the ship alongside a dock. You have the power and control, the hazard of messing up and the joy of doing it right. When it was safe to do so, I would let my officers try it, and they could share in the fun. First they would bring it alongside a box. Then, if I thought they knew how, they would make an actual landing. It was part of my philosophy of management—high standards but enjoy yourself.

Paul Stillwell: Did the Navy seem interested in getting any publicity for the achievements of the black crew?

Commander Meyer: I was not aware. I don't think so. You see, the war in Europe had just ended.[*] They were getting set for the rest of the war in the Pacific. The first assignment we got was that they wanted to test some brand-new depth charges which would be set off at the sound of a submarine's propellers. They wanted to see whether these depth charges would be set off by the surface ship's propellers as they were sinking down to the sub. As I have reflected since, if one of those weapons we were testing had failed and gone off prematurely, I wouldn't be here. The whole goddamn ship could have sunk.

With the attitude that the Navy had, I wouldn't be surprised if they said, "Oh, that ship, that black ship isn't worth a damn anyway. If we blow it up, what have we lost?

---

[*] V-E Day – Victory in Europe Day, 8 May 1945, when the German surrender was ratified in Berlin.

Let's let them test these things." These were 300-pound depth charges. That's a hell of a load for even a big man. We had 200 of them on board and dumped one after the other into the sea off Atlantic City, killing fish by the thousands and thousands. But we did it successfully and came back in to do it again the next day. That's when we got a letter commending us for that performance. I think it began to open some people's eyes.

Paul Stillwell: Well, specifically, I looked up your action report yesterday, your war diary on that.* On the 28th of June, you dropped 192 depth charges set at varying depths from 50 to 1,400 feet, and 50 feet is mighty shallow. They were fired from the stern projectors. Then on the 29th of June, the following day, you tested 225 Mark 14 depth charges, and that resulted in considerable superficial damage to the ship. So indeed there was the potential for harm.

Commander Meyer: Yes. Yes.

Paul Stillwell: Do you remember the damage?

Commander Meyer: No, and it never occurred to me that we could get killed or blown up. This was a job, and you do what you're told. A lot of guys had been killed in the Pacific.

Paul Stillwell: Well, and you had hoped that despite the feelings about the blacks that they wouldn't deliberately send you to do something that had that kind of potential.

Commander Meyer: I think the Navy had confidence that these depth charges would work, but they did want to prove them out. I think at the time I was glad to have a chance to show what we could do—you know, a chance to get out in the football field and play a game.

---

* The war diary of the USS *Mason* is on file in the National Archives branch in College Park, Maryland.

Paul Stillwell: Well, this was probably the closest you could come to a combat-type mission with the war being over in the Atlantic.

Commander Meyer: Yes.

Paul Stillwell: Well, after that, you proceeded the following week to Casco Bay along with other ships of the division and did some refresher training from Destroyer Force Atlantic. What do you recall about that?

Commander Meyer: I do not have any recollection about our period of training in Casco Bay, except for one screwy idea I had. During almost two years on that staff in Hawaii, I had been much involved in training ships to provide gunfire support to Marines and the Army as they assaulted Jap-held islands. I got the idea to do something of the same up there. I was going to put some observers ashore to spot the gunfire for us. Of course, it would have been a foolish and hazardous thing to do. John Phillips wisely said, "Captain, I don't think this is a good idea." I was the captain, but fortunately I could listen, and I had people who would speak up.

So I remember going to Casco Bay, but I don't remember in particular what we things did.

Paul Stillwell: Well, let me just run through them. On the 11th of July you had ship handling and general drills; the 12th, tactical maneuvers—towing, breeches buoy, visit and search, underwater damage control; 13th was ASW; 16th was antiaircraft firing, damage control, and night illumination.* So you really spanned the spectrum there.

Commander Meyer: Yes.

Paul Stillwell: Had there been some turnover in crew that brought on this need for refresher training?

---

* ASW – antisubmarine warfare.

Commander Meyer: There always is a little turnover. No, I just felt we needed the training. See, we were gung ho to go to the Pacific and fight the Japs. I wanted our ship to be in top-notch shape, so we just drilled like a good football team.

Paul Stillwell: Did the *Mason* spend enough time in port while you were in command for you to have an idea of the liberty opportunities for the black crew members?

Commander Meyer: Well, the North was okay, and, of course, a lot of the crew seemed to have come from New York City, or had their families in New York. Of course, in the years since, people have talked about mixed marriages and so on and so on. Well, I saw white women come down and meet their black husbands, and they seemed just as happy as the blacks that I saw. As long as we were up north, liberty was fine. The minute we got south, it was different. For instance, there was an incident when we were scrimmaging with a submarine on evasive tactics out of Port Everglades, Florida, which is right at Fort Lauderdale. Hell, in those days a Jew had better not be overnight in Lauderdale, much less a black man.

At every southern port I'd go to, I remember that the minute the lines were tied up, I'd jump ashore and go to the police department, because in those days white policemen down South were a pretty scruffy, prejudiced lot. I'd say, "Look, I'm in here with this crew; my crew's been out fighting the war. They're not just steward's mates; they're not servants. They've been out fighting the war for you guys, and I expect them to be treated like American sailors. On the other hand, if any of them get out of line, you can count on me that I'll stand by you. If they're really out of line and commit some crimes, I'll back you up."

Well, one night about 2:00 A.M., some of the crew woke me up, saying, "Captain, Captain, Willie's going to get lynched. He's down at the police station. They're going to lynch him."

So I went down to the police station. They had one of our men there. It turns out at 1:00 o'clock in the morning, they'd been coming from a black section of town in a cab with about eight of them. Willie was at the bottom of this pile, hardly able to breathe, much less talk, see. A white woman walked across the street—a single white women in a town at 1:00 A.M. What the hell is she? Probably a whore. But the policeman said Willie had insulted her. So I got him back to the ship, and the next day is when I assembled them all on the dock, and I said, "This happened. I think it's unfair. Willie's back." But I said, "You know, we're in southern territory. We're just going to have to be more pure than pure. If we have any incidents where anybody steps out of line, I'll restrict the whole damn ship, and you won't have any liberty."

I've often thought that's when some of the men gave me the nickname of "the warden," which among black people is really not a term of endearment. But I made it very clear, and there were no more incidents.

Then when we were decommissioning at the Charleston Navy Yard, I insisted that Jim Hair and McIntosh, the two black officers, come with me to the officers' club.* I said, "Goddamnit, you're officers and you have a right to go to the club, and I insist."

"Aw," they said, "we don't want to go to the officers' club, Captain. It will get you in trouble."

I said, "I insist you come over." So we came and sat in very conspicuous seats. Service just about stopped, because all the service people were black; they were amazed. After we'd had one drink, Jim said, "Well, Captain, you've had your fun now. Could we please excuse ourselves and go to our part of town, where we can have a good time and you stay here?"

So I think they had the opportunity for recreation, but of their own kind.

Paul Stillwell: Well, with the "warden" nickname you were the focus for the resentment that really should have been directed elsewhere.

Commander Meyer: Oh, I suppose. Some of the guys, I'm sure, thought I was just great, and some of them thought, "Who's this honky?" And I didn't care. I dropped out of the popularity contest about 50 years ago.

---

* The *Mason* arrived at Charleston, South Carolina, on 10 September 1945 and was decommissioned there on 12 October 1945.

Paul Stillwell: Well, did you develop any more than superficial relationships with some of the crew?

Commander Meyer: Well, it's hard to say, Paul, because, you know, it was only three months—three very busy months. We were busy, and we had those projects. On the one hand, I have this great reverence and respect for enlisted men. Yet I knew from the Naval Academy that there should always be this gulf. You know, it's unfair to enlisted men for officers to hang around with them.

When we went to Charleston Navy Yard, of course, the first thing they came to me and said, "Captain, we're being 'Jim Crowed' at the movie theater on the Navy yard."* So I went to the officer in charge.

He said, "That's wrong. Your men have been out there. They should sit where they want to sit, anywhere."

Turns out one of the petty officers at the door had said, "You black men sit in the last row of the balcony." And then, to my surprise, I found out my men had been swimming in the Navy yard pool with white women and white people, and nothing happened. So I don't know. I sort of insisted on their rights, which I thought was their due.

Paul Stillwell: You told me a story before the tape started that bears repeating and that's Hair's experience at a hotel.

Commander Meyer: Well, I wanted him to go to damage control school in Philadelphia for a month and stay at the Adelphia Hotel, which is a very, very nice hotel where they wouldn't let a black man in the back door except as a janitor. But they had to let him in because he was a naval officer. When he came back, of course, I was interested in how he'd been treated, so I said, "Jim, how'd they treat you?"

He said, "Oh, fine, they thought I was an Italian."

---

* Thomas D. Rice, a black minstrel singer, wrote a song and dance titled "Jim Crow" in 1832. Later in the century, the term took on the meaning of segregation of the races, as in "Jim Crow laws."

The great thing you'll find out from Jim Hair, he's got a real, real sense of humor and no bitterness. He's very conscious of the fact that blacks have been pushed around, but he doesn't brood on it. Inasmuch as a black man and a white man could, he and I communed about it. I resent the way some people have been treated—blacks, Jews, women, or Mexicans.

The *Mason* was this watershed in my life. I got into civil rights. I worked in Jersey. I got to know Duke Ellington and he put on a concert, benefit concert for us.[*] We made 7,500 bucks in that one night in our church. When I met Duke the first time, he kissed me four times. I said, "Why four times?"

He said, "Once for each cheek." A wonderful guy.

I no more than got back from the war than Union Carbide, which had bought Bakelite, wanted to start a company and a factory in Mexico. I was sent down to establish and run it. I got to know Mexicans who, of course, had been subject to discrimination. They're damn smart, hard-working people, really, except for their politicians, which isn't much different from a few other places.

Then I've worked in Peru for a while. And I've had a very, very fortunate life except for these depressions. I've had about five depressions; they've all been job related. One of them I wound up in the psychiatric ward at Presbyterian Hospital in New York City for a week. Very, very interesting week. I wouldn't wish it on anybody.

Paul Stillwell: Did you inspect the crew and the messing and berthing while you were captain?

Commander Meyer: Oh, yes. As a matter of fact, I remember once toward the end of the war I said, "John, let's write an article for *The Saturday Evening Post*. At that time, people "knew" black people had unusual body odor. I was going to say, "That isn't so. The quarters are clean and the men are clean." He said, "Captain, you're going to write an article about body odor?" He talked me out of that one.

But we took white officers from the Subchaser Training Center Key West through for a week at a time to give them their practice. We cleared out one crew's quarters, and

---

[*] Edward Kennedy "Duke" Ellington (1899-1974) was a noted black pianist, bandleader, and composer.

they lived there. The officers had their own head. There were no incidents. As a matter of fact, at the end of one week, the officers were filing off the ship and an officer with a very deep Georgia accent came over. He said, "Captain, when they assigned me to this ship, I almost refused to go. I wasn't going to go on any black ship." And he said, "I realized in wartime you just don't do that. I want you to know how much I appreciate this week. It's a revelation. Your gunner's mates and others gave us lectures. They knew their jobs, they spoke very clearly, and they were good instructors. The men had a good time, and we visited."

You've asked me about whether I got a fair shake on the crew. I don't know, I thought they had the potential. We got rid of those that didn't. And the ones that stayed sure as hell performed.

Rupe Lowe, this Navy guy that I worked for in Union Carbide—one of his great sayings was, "People will fly up to meet your expectations." If you think well of people's potential, they'll do the goddamnedest to be sure you're not disappointed in the faith that you've had in them. It's a tremendously powerful motivator, and blacks aren't any different than anybody else. If you think they're going to perform, and you expect them and give them the break, they'll bust their gut.

Paul Stillwell: And the reverse can be true as well.

Commander Meyer: Oh, yes. If you think they're shit, they'll just do the least possible. Sure they will. That's the great romance in management—I've been a manager all my life—to see how people grow, grow and fly, and perform.

Paul Stillwell: Maybe we could talk a bit more about your role there in Florida.

Commander Meyer: Well, we were doing this training—and I don't know how many weeks it was. I guess I'd better get over to Washington and read those diaries.[*]

---

[*] At the time of the interviews, the wartime records for the *Mason* were archived at the Naval Historical Center in Washington, D.C.

Paul Stillwell: Did you have live submarines to work against?

Commander Meyer: There were these two episodes. One was taking these students out, where we would let them fire a gun and experience the engineering spaces. We were just a school ship for them. And, as I say, it was a very satisfactory—because my crew by then was well trained and proud to be a school ship.

The other one we were going down to Miami, this is in time reverse—going by Port Everglades, and a destroyer escort and a submarine had been practicing for months. The submarine was developing evasive tactics to use against the Japanese surface ships. And they said, "Well, we need some fresh bait that hasn't been subjected to these evasions, to see how effective they are."

We were going down the coast at that time, so they diverted us to go in and be the target ship. The first day the sub was ten miles away and told that it had to constrain its movements within, say, a two-mile-wide corridor, and we were to try to find it. We found it, as our sonar crew was really superb. So the next day, the sub had more latitude, and we found it again. Finally, I think the last day was real graduation day. By now, pride, you know. We were going to show them how good we were. You see, when you get contact with a sub, the sonar man is sending the signal, "beep, beep, beep," and if he gets an echo back, he yells, "Contact."

And you yell, "Bearing."

You have this staccato language so that you don't say, "Gee, what's he doing out there?"

"I don't know what, Captain." And by then he's gone, see. And this was graduation day, because the sub was free to do anything he wanted to, and we were going to catch him. "Beep, beep, beep, beep, bong."

Instead of saying, "Contact," he said, "Who dat?"

Well, I knew what he meant. I guess he got away eventually. I went ashore to the captain in charge and I said, "Well, Captain, I'm sorry that we goofed up the last day with the ship got—the sub got away from us."

He said, "It's a goddamned good thing. You had his morale down at the bottom of the ocean. He couldn't get away from your crew." So that was a happy, happy week.

And, of course, it's the week when the police were going to lynch Willie, or had him in tow.

Then we went down to Miami to be a school ship.[*] And then the last week, we got under way Monday morning. Of course, the first days on board were busy as hell with drills. That night at 9:00 o'clock I finally got to my cabin and was reading the mail that had come aboard. I knew that, as a lieutenant commander, I was about at the seniority where I might be selected for a commander. I looked at the book, and damn it, I was not on the list. I said, "Damn shore-based bastards got all the promotions." Then I looked again, and I had been promoted. So that was Monday.

Tuesday, I learned that the A-bomb had been dropped, so we knew the war was going to end, or something.[†] Wednesday I got orders to come ashore and abort the whole week of training because the war was nearly over. And Thursday we had orders to go up to New London, Connecticut, where my wife and little three-year old child were. So it was a week or two of too much good news to stand.

Naturally, I was pleased with the promotion. When I was a lieutenant commander people would say, "Commander."

And I'd say, "No, I'm not a commander; I'm a lieutenant commander. Call me a lieutenant commander—or mister—I don't want to pretend to be a commander."

Then when I made commander, a couple of things happened. They'd say, "Commander. You mean you're a lieutenant commander because you're so young?"

"No," I said, "I have three stripes." Before I used to always wear the "go-to-hell" cloth cap. I'd see these guys—the minute they made commander, they'd get the cap with the spinach on it.[‡] Well, I decided I'd get one of those, but they were all bought up. When I finally got one on, I found out they were very effective: "Yes, Commander. No, Commander. What would you like, Commander?" Open the doors, and so on.

---

[*] Subchaser Training School, Miami, Florida.
[†] B-29 bombers of the U.S. Army Air Forces dropped atomic bombs on Hiroshima, Japan, on 6 August 1945 and on Nagasaki, Japan, on 9 August 1945. The Japanese surrendered shortly afterward.
[‡] The commander's combination cap has a black visor decorated with a pattern of gold leaves. The visor on a lieutenant commander's cap is all black. The decorative gold is often referred to as "scrambled eggs" or "spinach."

During that week of the VJ Day, we had several of our men ashore in Miami on shore patrol.* First there was a false report that the Japanese war had ended. Somehow, during the jubilation the mob in Miami got out of hand and started to attack four white members of a shore patrol group and were beating up on two of them. Two of their buddies escaped—running for their own hide. Two of the *Mason*'s black shore patrolmen waded in and rescued the two white men. They got a letter commending them for something I thought was a pretty damn good performance of duty.

That was one of four letters of commendation that we got. The first was for the sonic depth charges; the second one was the submarine evasive tactics; the third was for the members of our shore patrol; and the fourth was dropping those ten-pound depth charges in an underwater signaling test.

Paul Stillwell: Well, four in three months is a pretty good record.

Commander Meyer: Well, I thought so.

Paul Stillwell: Please tell me more about the signaling tests.

Commander Meyer: After our trip to New London, we went to Bermuda for these tests. We used little ten-pound depth charges. They sink to a layer of the sea about 3,000 feet down, and because of the temperature differential, sound travels fantastic distances. This was before the days of modern navigation and so on. The plan was that every transatlantic steamer or transatlantic airplane would carry one of these. If they went down, they'd drop it, and we had listening posts in Portugal, Halifax, and Florida. If they heard the sound of this, they could triangulate and tell whether there's somebody out there at that position. We tested it.

While we were at Hamilton, Bermuda, we almost ruined all of our good reputation. John Phillips was not great at navigation. We were steaming away, and all of a sudden, the previous exec, who was still on board as a passenger, rushed up and said, "Captain, you're going to run aground. The harbor entrance is here, and the lighthouse is

---

* VJ Day – Victory over Japan, 14 August 1945.

flashing danger." Fortunately, we were warned off, or we would have impaled ourselves on the rocks, which, of course, people would have said, "There's that goddamned, no-good black ship . . ." It would have ruined all that we were trying to do.

Paul Stillwell: Did you feel a sense of being a missionary?

Commander Meyer: Oh, sure, oh, sure. I was a crusader, missionary, whatever you want to call it. I've always been a crusader. When I later worked for Union Carbide, I tried to get jobs for black secretaries, or see that Jews got a fair break. Yes, I undertook to do what I thought was decent and right.

I took the Declaration of Independence seriously.

Paul Stillwell: Well, and you can do some effective things in officers' clubs, for example. Just spread the word.

Commander Meyer: Oh, yes. People would say, "You know how Negroes are."

I'd say, "Do you really?" And I would just quietly tell them. Or somebody'd talk about niggers, and I'd say, "Sorry, but you're talking about some of the best friends that I have," which is true, without beating them over the head with it. I would just say, "I don't believe in that. This has been my experience."

Sure, I've been a crusader all my life, and proud of it.

Paul Stillwell: One of the things that Admiral Zumwalt did was specifically raise consciousness about items of black culture, putting things in exchanges, on the menus.[*]

Did you find yourself in any way adapting to black culture on board the ship?

Commander Meyer: Well, only to the degree that I got used to living in a black world, where almost everybody I looked at was black. The thing as when I moved to Mexico—

---

[*] Admiral Elmo R. Zumwalt, Jr., USN, was Chief of Naval Operation from 1970 to 1974. During that time he initiated a number of programs on behalf of black naval personnel.

they're sort of swarthy, and mustaches are very, very common. It just became commonplace. After a while, you're not sensitive to it. That's the way that world is.

Other than that, the music that the crew played was strictly their kind of music, as much as they could. I didn't try to play my Bach and Beethoven records. I didn't think they'd get across very well.

Paul Stillwell: Were there any language specialties or customs that your crew practiced that you found unusual from other ships?

Commander Meyer: I don't think so, because these were guys that had been through high school at least. They were just a good crew and that made them better, I'd say. We gave them a chance to fly, and I felt very proud

Paul Stillwell: When did you leave the ship?

Commander Meyer: Of course, the minute the war was over, I was ready to leave. I'd been in since March of '41; I'd been overseas three and a half years. I had what they called "points," and I got out just as fast as I could go.* I turned the ship over to John Phillips and arrived home to my wife Thursday night. Monday morning I was back in my old job in Bakelite.

Paul Stillwell: Had you given any thought to trying to get a regular commission, or was that an option?

Commander Meyer: It was an option. I could have stayed in and ranked with the class of '37, but I knew that there would always be that little tick, "Meyer doesn't have good eyesight." Anyhow, I was intensely proud. People used to say, "What's Bakelite, a religion?" Because I was very, very proud of the factory that I'd come from, and the people, and this boss out of '22 that I had worked for. The Navy was great, and when

---

* A system of points was set up to determine priority of demobilization. Because of his length and type of service, Commander Meyer had a large number of the necessary points.

they autopsy me, they're going to find my blood is not red; it's navy blue and gold spiral like this spiral toothpaste you see. But I was glad to get out. I'd done my part to repay my education to Uncle Sam.

Paul Stillwell: You talked about the decommissioning of the *Mason*. Were you present for that?

Commander Meyer: No. John Phillips handled it. By then, it was just going through a routine. I was not needed at all anymore.

Paul Stillwell: So it was pretty anticlimactic by that point.

Commander Meyer: Oh, yes. The war was over and BOOM!, people scattered.

Paul Stillwell: Well, I think, a problem that you didn't have that some veterans might have was that you didn't have to start over when you got out. You were really just resuming what you had done before, so that helped the transition considerably.

Commander Meyer: Oh, yes. They wanted me back, and I had a good job—made 350 bucks a month, every month. But we worked six days a week, so I got a raise.

I remember when I was general manager of that company in Mexico. I finally got up to $10,000 a year—big money in '52.

Paul Stillwell: What are some of the highlights of your time since the war?

Commander Meyer: Well, of course, being the general manager of that company in Mexico was a great thing, because I was still a young kid. I was in my 30s, then just turned 40. My boss was very busy, with the big company in the States, and by then he and I had big brother-little brother rapport. So I had a great deal of independence and autonomy down there to run the company. I loved the Mexicans. My wife and I both learned the language. We were Protestant Americans in a Catholic country, but after a while the Mexicans sensed that we liked them. We were invited to parties and social functions that other Americans didn't even know existed. We spoke the language, and so that was certainly a highlight.

Paul Stillwell: What products did the factory make?

Commander Meyer: Well, we manufactured what is called Bakelite, the old phenol-formaldehyde molding material, and later on polystyrene was the second product line that we put in. But then we also imported products in our warehouse and sold it. Then we also ordered, in effect, through a catalog.

When I went to the Naval Academy, I wanted to study German. I was given this oral quiz, and the old professor said, "Young man, you're so stupid. You study German, you go home in three months. Study something easy like Spanish. Maybe you stay." Fortunately, I studied Spanish, so when I went to Mexico, it wasn't too hard. I remember the company had made a terrible mistake in going there in the first place. But we pulled it out.

But I was not only general manager and the chief engineer, and so on, but I was a salesman and a collector, and everything else too. I went to Benny Cavazos, I remember, to tell him about the products—the different colors and so on—all in halting Spanish. He didn't speak a word of English. Then I had to go back the next day with some other things that I didn't have with me. The next day he spoke English perfectly. Later, when we got to be good friends, I said, "Benny, that was a dirty trick."

"Well," he said, "you come into my country to make a living in my country. I thought you ought to speak our language. You struggled, but you made it." And that was a highlight.

Then, you see, Union Carbide was going to make me the vice president in charge of all of Latin America—Mexico, Central and South America—six factories. They were going to divide the world up into three zones: America, Asia, and Europe. I was going to be this big one. I turned them down because I didn't like the foreign department's ethics in business. Probably should have, you know. I could have gotten in and had an influence on them. But I said, "No, I'm going to go back and work for this Navy guy.

Trouble is that was Wednesday, and Friday he was, in effect, kicked upstairs. So I had my flag on the wrong flagpole.

I stayed with Union Carbide ten more years. Then I left and went to Peru with ITT, ran into a Communist union, and damn near got killed.* The kids nearly got shot.

Then I was out of work for ten and a half months. So my fortunes changed a great deal. I had been one of the bright guys at Union Carbide, but I stepped off the boat. I went through bad times, and then got the job by answering a *New York Times* want ad, "Hospital Personnel Director." Got a job at Roosevelt Hospital in New York City, and at the end of four years got fired—difference in philosophy. But I'd picked up this job running a little hospital in New Mexico. Then 12 years ago, I was asked to come up to this great big center as one of the administrators.

Getting back, running my own hospital, and now my present job is great. I get ten weeks off a year paid; it's more time off than you can afford. So I can travel like crazy. Our kids are all grown and successful in their professions. My wife and I are going to spend Thanksgiving skiing in Colorado. We're in good health.

I've gone 18 backpacks into the Grand Canyon. You know, I've got these genes, and I just haven't stopped. I just keep in shape.

Paul Stillwell: What is your present job?

Commander Meyer: Well, really, I'm a contract consultant. But I handle the complaints—malpractice suits, and so on. People say, "Yuk, what a job!"

But all my life, see, I've been a troubleshooter. I've always gone into different jobs—even at Union Carbide. I went to Mexico. I came back and, "This is in trouble, and that," and so on. And that hospital in Silver City was in a muddle when I took it on. When people have serious complaints, they're referred to me, and I have enough status and independence to settle a great deal of things. Things do go wrong. Medicine is a very iffy business. But if we get sued, why, they turn it over to me.

But most people are reasonable. I have a great deal of independence to resolve disputes right then and there—$10,000 write-off. I do it. The other day I wrote off

---

* ITT – International Telephone & Telegraph.

$14,000, because we were going to experiment with this guy, and the experiment didn't turn out. He had long-term suffering but ran up a $14,000 bill, and I just wrote it off.

I'm well paid and well treated. And I've got a wonderful wife. She and I have been married for 45 years—meaningful, happy, adventuresome years. And our kids and grandchildren have always meant a great deal to us. You know, it's hard to say what was the high point.

Paul, I've just been a very lucky guy, including emerging from that year out of work and then the depressions that I've been through. I got in good hands and got out of them, survived and fat and happy. So I'm a pretty damn lucky guy.

Paul Stillwell: Well, I appreciate your taking the time to share your experiences here. Your work is a legacy to the present generation of black sailors in the Navy—paving the way for them. And to have it recorded will, undoubtedly, be of value to future generations.

Commander Meyer: Well, I hope so. It just proved how capable they could be if they're given the opportunity and the leadership. I think that's all. And that blacks are people—you know, that great, profound truth—blacks are people. So what's new?

Launched in 1969, the U.S. Naval Institute's award-winning oral history program is among the oldest in the country. Used in combination with documentary sources, oral histories offer a richer understanding of naval history through candid recollections and explanations rarely entered into contemporary records. In addition, they help depict the atmosphere of a particular event or era in a manner not available in official documents.

The nonprofit Naval Institute accomplishes its history projects through contributed funds and gratefully accepts tax-deductible gifts of all sizes for this purpose. This support allows the Institute to preserve the life experiences of today's service men and women so they may enlighten and inspire future generations.

For information about opportunities to underwrite Naval Institute oral history projects, please contact the Naval Institute Foundation at 291 Wood Road, Annapolis, Maryland 21402; by phone at (410) 295-1054; or by e-mail at foundation@usni.org.

Index to the Oral History of
Commander Norman H. Meyer, U.S. Naval Reserve (Retired)

Antisubmarine Warfare
    The corvette *Saucy* (PG-65) patrolled in World War II in the Atlantic, 9-12
    Depth charge tests by the destroyer escort *Mason* (DE-529) in 1945, 24-25, 34
    The Subchaser Training School at Key West, Florida, provided ASW instruction in the summer of 1945, 30-32
    ASW exercises off the Florida coast in the summer of 1945, 32-33

Baker, Rear Admiral Wilder D., USN (USNA, 1914)
    In 1942 counseled Meyer, who was having trouble adjusting to duty in the corvette *Saucy* (PG-65), 10
    In 1944-45 was chief of staff to Vice Admiral John S. McCain, 13

Barham, Rear Admiral Eugene A., USN (Ret.) (USNA, 1935)
    Served as regimental commander while a midshipman at the Naval Academy in the early 1930s, 3-4

Charleston Navy Yard, Charleston, South Carolina
    Racial issues in 1945 when the destroyer escort *Mason* (DE-529) was in the shipyard, 28-29

Depth Charges
    Tests by the destroyer escort *Mason* (DE-529) in 1945, 24-25, 34

Disciplinary Problems
    Captain's mast on board the destroyer escort *Mason* (DE-529) in 1945, 18

Enlisted Personnel
    Crew members of the corvette *Saucy* (PG-65) in World War II, 11-12, 22
    Crew members of the destroyer escort *Mason* (DE-529) in 1945, 8, 15-36

Fahy, Commander Edward J., USN (USNA, 1934)
    In 1945 was a detailer in the Bureau of Naval Personnel, 14, 17

Hair, James E.
    In 1945 commanded the yard tugboat *YTB-215* and was later in the crew of the destroyer escort *Mason* (DE-529), 17, 20-21, 28-30

Leave and Liberty
    Problems for black crew members of the destroyer escort *Mason* (DE-529) in southern liberty ports in 1945, 27-29

Lowe, Midshipman Rupert B., USN (USNA, 1922)
    Graduated from the Naval Academy in 1922 but elected to resign rather than take a commission and subsequently worked for Bakelite and Union Carbide, 5, 31, 36, 38

***Mason*, USS (DE-529)**
    When commissioned in 1944, initially had a crew of white officers and black enlisted men, later got black officers, 8, 15-36
    Operations in the Atlantic in the summer of 1945, 7-8, 16-36
    Problems for the *Mason*'s black crew members in southern liberty ports in 1945, 27-29

McGowan, Lieutenant (junior grade) Richard, USN (USNA, 1935)
    In 1941 persuaded his former Naval Academy roommate, Meyer, to teach aviation cadets about the Navy, 7

McIntosh, Ensign John, USNR
    Among the relatively few black naval officers commissioned in World War II, he served on board the destroyer escort *Mason* (DE-529), 21, 28

Medical Problems
    Over the years Meyer was treated for depression, 9-11, 30

Meyer, Commander Norman H., USNR (Ret.)
    Parents, 1-4
    Siblings, 1-3
    Wife Barbara, 7-10, 33, 37, 40
    Youth in Minnesota in the 1910s-30s, 1-4
    As a Naval Academy midshipman, 1931-35, 2-5
    Served as a junior officer at sea, 1935-37, 5
    Released from active duty because of vision problems, 5-7
    Worked 1937-41 as a process engineer at the Bakelite Corporation in New Jersey, 5-6, 23
    Returned to active duty in March 1941 to teach aviation cadets at Pensacola, 7-9, 20
    In 1942-43 served as executive officer and then commanding officer of the corvette *Saucy* (PG-65), 9-12
    From 1943 to 1945 was on the staff of Commander Cruisers Pacific Fleet and Commander Destroyers Pacific Fleet, 12-13
    For a few months in 1945 commanded the destroyer escort *Mason* (DE-529), 7-8, 15-36
    Post-World War II civilian employment, 30, 35-40

Myrdal, Gunnar
    In 1944 published the book *An American Dilemma: The Negro Problem and Modern Democracy*, 13-14

Naval Academy, Annapolis, Maryland
Medical requirements for admission in 1931, 2-3
Regimental leadership in the early 1930s, 3-4
Academics in the early 1930s, 4-5

Navigation
In 1945 the destroyer escort *Mason* (DE-529) had navigation problems in the port of Hamilton, Bermuda, 34-35

O'Handley, Captain John G., USN (Ret.) (USNA, 1935)
Roomed with Meyer four years at the Naval Academy in the 1930s, 2, 14

Phillips, Lieutenant (junior grade) John C., USNR
Served as executive officer on board the destroyer escort *Mason* (DE-529) in 1945, 16-20, 24, 26, 30, 34-37
Civilian career after World War II, 20-21

Racial Issues
Black employees at the Naval Academy in the early 1930s, 14-15
In 1944 Swedish economist Gunnar Myrdal published the book *An American Dilemma: The Negro Problem and Modern Democracy*, 13-14
Attitudes toward black Navy personnel during World War II, 14-15
When commissioned in 1944, the destroyer escort *Mason* (DE-529) initially had a crew of white officers and black enlisted men, later got black officers, 8, 15-36
Problems for the *Mason*'s black crew members in southern liberty ports in 1945, 27-29, 32-34

Saucy, USS (PG-65)
Corvette commissioned in 1942 in Ireland for antisubmarine service in the U.S. Navy, 9-12, 22
Enlisted crew members in World War II, 11-12, 22

Seager, Commander John W., SC, USN (Ret.)
Was originally in the Naval Academy class of 1932, later resigned from the academy and became a supply officer, 2. 15

Shaffer, Rear Admiral J. Nevin, USN (Ret.) (USNA, 1935)
Served as regimental commander as a Naval Academy midshipman in 1934-35, 4

Smith, Lieutenant Andrew J., USN (USNA, 1931)
In 1942-43 commanded the corvette *Saucy* (PG-65), 9-11

Subchaser Training School, Key West, Florida
Antisubmarine training in the summer of 1945, 30-31

www.ingramcontent.com/pod-product-compliance
Lightning Source LLC
Chambersburg PA
CBHW080609170426
43209CB00007B/1378